Information Systems En

Management of Software Maintenance

Dave O'Neill
Richard West

CCTA

July 1993

LONDON: HMSO

© Crown Copyright 1993

Applications for reproduction should be made to HMSO

First published 1993

ISBN 0 11 330584 2

ISSN 0967-9561

For further information regarding this publication and other CCTA products please contact:

CCTA Library
Riverwalk House
157-161 Millbank
London SW1P 4RT

071-217-3331

Contents

Foreword

1 **Introduction**   1

    1.1   Purpose

    1.2   Who should read this guide

    1.3   Background

    1.4   Structure of this guide

2 **Overview**   3

3 **Definition and categories of maintenance**   7

    3.1   Importance of software maintenance

    3.2   Definition of software maintenance

    3.3   Types of application

    3.4   Categories of software maintenance

    3.5   Maintenance statistics

    3.6   Maintenance in the information system lifecycle

4 **Scope, risks and costs of maintenance**   13

    4.1   Scope of software maintenance

    4.2   Maintenance risks

    4.3   Cost of maintenance

5	**IS strategy and policies**		**23**
	5.1	IS strategy and software maintenance	
	5.2	Maintenance portfolio	
	5.3	Management and technical policies	
	5.4	Special policies for old systems	
	5.5	Original analysis, design, development and testing	
	5.6	Further advice	
6	**Processes and organisation**		**31**
	6.1	Problem management	
	6.2	Change management	
	6.3	Configuration management	
	6.4	Change control procedures	
	6.5	Emergency changes	
	6.6	Release control	
	6.7	Post implementation review	
	6.8	Prioritisation of maintenance activity	
	6.9	Allocation of appropriate resources	
	6.10	Organisation of a maintenance unit	
	6.11	Further advice	

7	**Testing**		**41**
	7.1	Development practices	
	7.2	Amendment testing	
	7.3	Regression testing	
	7.4	Risks associated with limited testing	
	7.5	Sign off	
	7.6	Further advice	
8	**Control and review of software systems**		**47**
	8.1	Need for reviews	
	8.2	Activity measurement	
	8.3	System audits	
	8.4	Control actions	
	8.5	Feedback to software developers	
9	**Contracting out software maintenance**		**53**
	9.1	Issues and risks	
	9.2	Benefits	
	9.3	Further advice	

10	**Software maintenance services at arm's length**		**61**
	10.1	Provision of services at arm's length	
	10.2	Statement of service requirement	
	10.3	Service agreement	
	10.4	Service monitoring	
Bibliography			**71**
Glossary			**75**

Foreword

The **Information Systems Engineering Library** provides guidance on managing and carrying out Information Systems Engineering activities. In the IS lifecycle, Information Systems Engineering takes place once the IS strategy has been defined. It is concerned with the development and ongoing improvement of information systems up to the operational stage, when systems become the responsibility of infrastructure management.

The Information Systems Engineering Library builds on guidance in the CCTA IS Guides, particularly set A: *Management and Planning Set* and set B: *Systems Development Set* and complements other CCTA products, in particular the project management method, PRINCE, and the systems analysis and design method, SSADM.

Volumes in the Information Systems Engineering Library are of interest to varying levels of staff from IS directors to IS providers, helping them to improve the quality and productivity of their IS development work. Some volumes in this library should also be of interest to business managers, IS users and those involved in market testing, whose business operations depend on having in place effective IS support by means of Information Systems Engineering activities.

The Information Systems Engineering Library also complements other related CCTA publications, particularly the IT Infrastructure Library for operational issues and the IS Planning Subject Guides for strategic issues.

CCTA welcomes customer views on Information Systems Engineering Library publications. Please send your comments to:

> Customer Services
> Information Systems Engineering Group
> Gildengate House
> Upper Green Lane
> Norwich NR3 1DW

Management of Software Maintenance

1 Introduction

1.1 Purpose

The purpose of this volume is toq explain to managers involved in the provision or use of information systems (IS) in government:

- the scope and importance of application software maintenance

- the key reasons why software maintenance must be managed effectively

- an approach to software maintenance that addresses the key issues of quality and value for money.

1.2 Who should read this guide

This volume is aimed at IS Directors and IT Managers and their equivalents in customer divisions. The volume will be of interest to those involved in the day-to-day management and implementation of software maintenance and may also be of interest to IS planners and business managers whose business is supported by computer application software.

1.3 Background

Business managers may be forgiven for wondering why so much is spent on the maintenance of software, which does not have moving parts that wear out. The answer is that most maintenance activity is actually change to address customers' evolving requirements, while a smaller proportion of maintenance activity is carried out to correct faults that are difficult to avoid during software development. This volume aims to help organisations understand maintenanace issues and get good maintenance services that offer value for money.

A number of independent surveys have shown that some two-thirds of the total lifecycle cost of a software system is expended on maintenance.

Software maintainers have not always been aware of the value to the IS customer organisation of the application systems under their control. Sometimes inadequate control of maintenance or development has resulted in poor reliability or maintainability of software.

Business managers and application users have not always been aware of the complexity of the software maintenance activity and the impact of their requests for changes to the software. In order to manage application software maintenance effectively, there has to be an understanding not only of the process of maintenance but also a knowledge of the business and its requirements. This volume addresses these issues.

1.4   Structure of this guide

This volume addresses the following issues:

- the different categories of software maintenance (Chapter 3)

- the scope of software maintenance and the risks and costs involved (Chapter 4)

- IS strategy and software maintenance (Chapter 5)

- processes and organisation (Chapter 6)

- software testing following maintenance (Chapter 7)

- the control and review of systems being maintained (Chapter 8)

- third party maintenance of application software (Chapter 9)

- provision of maintenance services at arm's length (Chapter 10).

Chapter 2 provides an overview of the volume.

2 Overview

Computer software represents a substantial investment of time and money and provides an underpinning of essential services and functions for an organisation's business. Software maintenance is the process by which:

- this investment is protected and the application software improved

- the quality of the software and its relevance to the IS customers is preserved as business needs change.

Therefore, software maintenance is a vital activity which must be managed and controlled effectively. It is too important to be afforded low priority, to be allocated poor calibre staff or to be under resourced.

This volume concentrates on the management, organisation and control of software maintenance. The guidance aims to help readers understand how to:

- reduce the risks of software failure

- improve the quality of both the software maintenance process and the maintained software

- extend the useful life of software

- understand and control the cost of software maintenance

- ensure that resources are allocated to the most cost-effective tasks.

Typically, two-thirds of the system lifecycle cost is spent on software maintenance which can be a complex activity requiring considerable skill to carry it out effectively. Chapter 3 defines what maintenance is, how it is categorised and how it fits into the Information System lifecycle. Chapter 4 outlines the scope of software maintenance and the risks and costs involved.

Chapter 5 describes how the customer organisation's IS strategy should set out its broad requirements for software maintenance and for the policies that it wishes to invoke to control the provision of software maintenance services.

Chapter 6 describes the processes needed to control software maintenance activity and indicates how operational service provision, processes such as those for problem management, change management and release control should be used.

All changes to computer software must be adequately specified, developed and tested before the amended programs are introduced into the live system. Chapter 7 outlines the procedures for testing which must be followed if run time system failures are to be minimised and data integrity is to be preserved.

As a result of continuing incremental change, application systems can become more difficult and expensive to maintain. Chapter 8 describes how the ongoing process of maintenance can be monitored and reviewed to obtain early warning of the need for remedial action including a complete rewrite where necessary.

Software maintenance may be carried out under contract by a third party. Chapter 9 covers the issues involved. The information in this chapter is likely to be of value when undertaking market testing of this area of work. An outline of an approach to the specification, agreement and monitoring of a maintenance service that is provided at arm's length from the customer organisation's business areas is given in Chapter 10.

As information systems are often at the centre of business operations computer software is important to the whole organisation. Software maintenance is not solely the responsibility of the programmers tasked with its implementation. It is the responsibility of all concerned on both the IS and business sides to ensure that software maintenance is carried out to the highest standards. These standards need to be established and implemented by IS customer and IS provider managers.

Whilst some costs and resources are needed to put the procedures recommended in this volume in place, these procedures will enable managers to take control and obtain a more efficient and effective software maintenance service because:

- only changes that are beneficial to the business will be made and such changes will be undertaken in a planned, prioritised, timely and controlled manner

- the disruption and cost to the business from run time failures and emergency corrections will be reduced

- there will be a reduction of wasted time and effort by both customers and maintenance providers, because the quality of service is better

- potential problems with software will be easier to detect in advance thus allowing preventive action to be taken

- it will be easier to operate the maintenance service on a planned basis and therefore easier to predict resource requirements

- software maintainability will be improved.

Further advice on improving the maintainability of software is given in the Information Systems Engineering Library volume: *Improving the Maintainability of Software*.

3 Definition and categories of maintenance

3.1 Importance of software maintenance

Software maintenance covers a range of activities undertaken to enhance and protect the investment made by an organisation in the software supporting its business objectives and activities.

Software maintenance is fundamentally important because it underpins the provision of operational IT services delivered in an environment of:

- changing business needs and requirements:
    - in the nature of the information system being supported by the application
    - in the quality of service required
- changes to the underlying system environment, network and hardware platforms.

3.2 Definition of software maintenance

Software maintenance is not solely concerned with the correction of bugs. The IEEE standard definition of software maintenance is:

Any modification of a software product after delivery, to correct faults, to improve performance or other attributes, or to adapt the product to a changed environment.
IEEE Standard P1219

For the purpose of this volume, the IEEE definition of software maintenance is used. It covers all changes to the software of an application system, including enhancements, after the original implementation and sign-off. Only the total redevelopment of the software is excluded.

3.3 Types of application

The advice given in this volume applies to application software, regardless of the type of application supported or the nature of the software, as the same software maintenance principles apply. It does not matter whether the application is administrative, operational, batch, online or realtime.

3.4 Categories of software maintenance

Software maintenance can be split into four categories which reflect broadly differing degrees of impact on the code and the logical and physical designs of the software.

3.4.1 Definitions of categories

The four categories are:

- perfective
- corrective
- adaptive
- preventive.

3.4.2 Perfective maintenance

Perfective maintenance is any modification or enhancement of the existing functionality or performance of application software.

It covers the whole range of alterations to the software that are undertaken to reflect changing business and user needs.

This activity can range from minor changes to a single module to the introduction of a totally new function requiring modification of many programs and/or the creation of completely new subsystems.

Because the user requirements are being changed, the existing logical and physical designs must be fully analysed and are likely to need alteration.

These enhancements account for the majority of software maintenance activity.

Chapter 3
Definition and categories of maintenance

3.4.3 Corrective maintenance

Corrective maintenance is the correction of processing, performance or implementation problems in application software.

It is the activity traditionally associated with software maintenance, bug fixing and error correction.

Although in the majority of cases corrective maintenance may only involve changes to the code, the existing logical and physical designs must always be analysed before making any changes.

If the error was in the original requirements specification or in the design, there is a possibility that the corrective maintenance may necessitate changes to the physical or logical design of the system.

There is a high risk that any changes to code that affect the original logical or physical structure will make subsequent maintenance increasingly difficult, error prone and costly. The danger is that the consistency and traceability of the original development is lost and the value of the effort expended on the use of a structured method discipline to ensure consistency is undermined.

3.4.4 Adaptive maintenance

Adaptive maintenance is the changes made to application software to adapt it for a change of the supporting environment, network or hardware platform.

It may be necessitated by any environmental change, from a minor upgrade to system software, to a major porting exercise to enable a move to a new computer system, platform or environment.

Adaptive maintenance may well include changes to the existing physical design as well as the code. For example, particular constraints and limitations in the existing technical system options may have been imposed by the previous supporting database, operating system environment or hardware. The constraints may have influenced the design chosen in the original development or in subsequent adaptions to it, and these need to be considered and re-evaluated in the changing circumstances.

| 3.4.5 | Preventive maintenance | Preventive maintenance is the action taken to make subsequent maintenance of application software more efficient and reliable.

It covers activities such as reverse engineering, restructuring the code to accommodate future changes or improve readability and adding explanatory comments to code and documentation.

Preventive maintenance is undertaken to make future maintenance more efficient and effective. It does not include making any changes as a result of other currently outstanding maintenance requirements. |
|---|---|---|
| 3.5 | **Maintenance statistics** | A survey, commissioned by CCTA in 1990, showed that the proportions of the relevant categories of software maintenance in government were:

    Perfective 60%

    Corrective 17%

    Adaptive 18%

    Preventive 5%

Later surveys in other market sectors have shown a very similar breakdown. These figures give managers an indication of relative costs of accommodating changing business requirements compared with correcting errors, supporting new underlying IT or making future maintenance easier. |
| 3.6 | **Maintenance in the information system lifecycle** | Software maintenance is a major element of the IS lifecycle.

The position of maintenance in the IS lifecycle is illustrated in a very simplistic form in Figure 1. |

Chapter 3
Definition and categories of maintenance

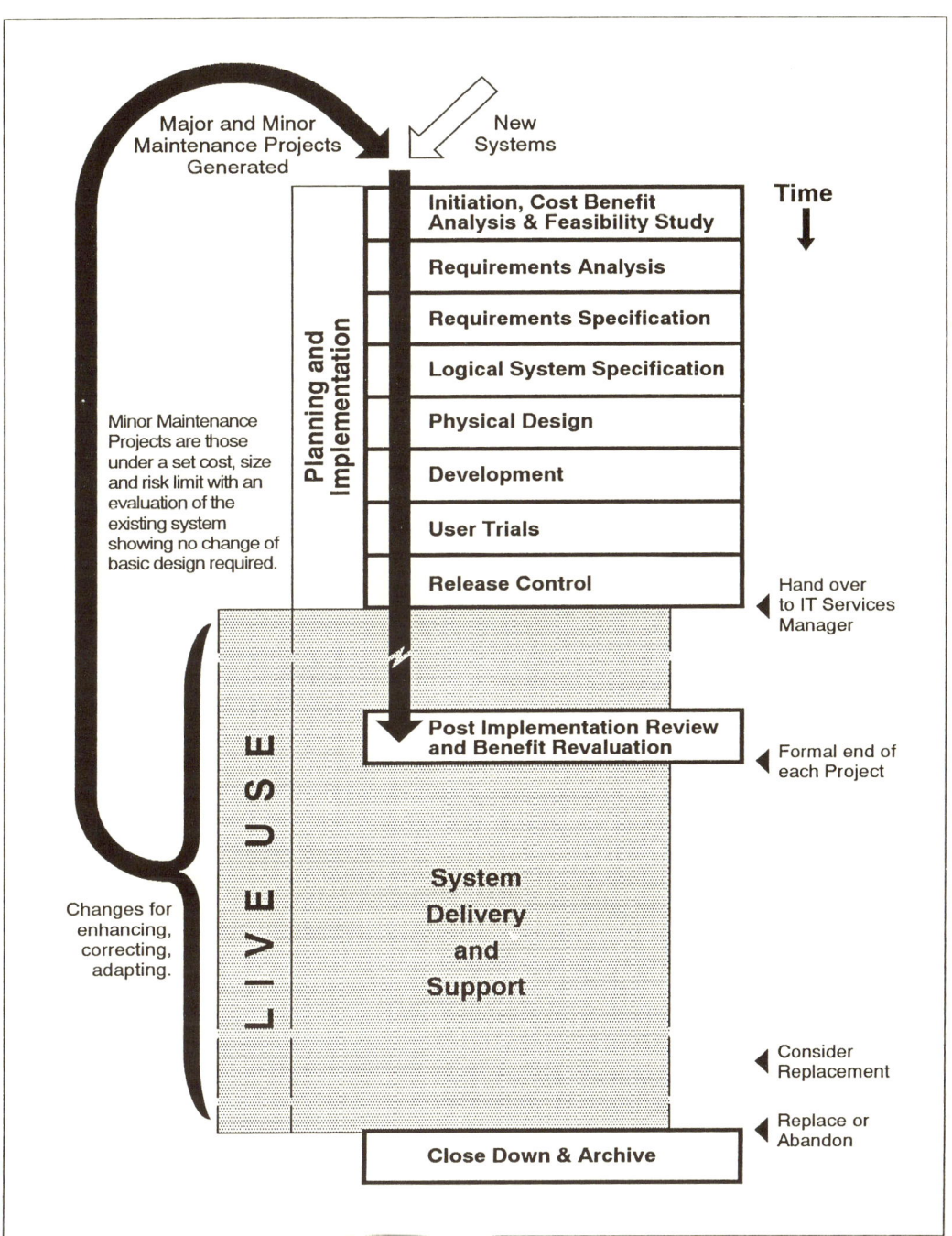

Figure 1: Maintenance in the IS project lifecycle

For clarity, the involvement of the business and users in verifying and testing the products of each stage is not shown in this figure nor are the critical functions of service delivery and support, such as the Help Desk, Problem Management or Change Management.

Software maintenance activities can range from major projects to minute changes. Superficially simple changes can have costly repercussions. The impact of proposed changes must be assessed and a decision must be taken on what is affected, for example, the original specification or the logical or physical design of the system.

To avoid problems associated with the impact of maintenance changes being insufficiently assessed, maintenance managers need to ensure that all proposed changes are assessed under formal change control and that no ill-informed assumptions are made in the impact assessment concerning how any particular correction or change may affect the rest of the system or the IT environment.

Maintenance changes should be implemented under project or change management control, the former if it is warranted by the cost, size and risk of the changes required. Even small-scale maintenance tasks that do not require any project control should still be managed under formal change management controls (see Chapter 6).

Lessons learnt from the post implementation review should be reflected back, as appropriate, to developers, maintainers and business managers.

4 Scope, risks and costs of maintenance

4.1 Scope of software maintenance

Changes to an organisation's software vary from minor alterations, for example changing the header on a report, to major changes to incorporate significant new functionality.

The original logical and physical design of an application software system are produced during the initial development, thus forming the software's structural framework which establishes:

- the functions to be performed by the software

- the sequence in which those functions are performed

- the internal dependencies and interrelationships

- communications with, for example, users, other programs or devices.

This framework having been agreed and established is then fleshed out with the software code which performs the required tasks.

During maintenance, the more significant the change, the more likely it is that the existing logical and physical designs will need to be amended rather than merely to alter the code. The need to change the logical and physical designs must be taken fully into account when making changes to software. Otherwise, the benefits and value of development using a structured method discipline are lost.

4.2 Maintenance risks

4.2.1 Categories of risk

Risks associated with software maintenance can be broadly categorised as follows:

- the software being maintained is of poor quality or ill-documented and therefore difficult to maintain

- the change to be made is expressed incorrectly or inadequately

- the financial case for the desired change has not been thought through

- the impact of the change and the activity involved in effecting it are not understood

- changes are made without altering all relevant documentation, for example, design documentation when design changes are made

- there are inadequate resources or skills or the maintainers are demotivated

- there are insufficient standards or procedures for maintainers to follow

- there are inadequate change-control procedures

- maintainers are under undue pressure to deliver to overly tight targets

- there is insufficient test data available

- customers' expectations are unrealistic

- the need for preventive maintenance is not recognised.

For pointers to guidance or discussion on the mitigation of these risks please refer to Figure 2.

Chapter 4
Scope, risks and costs of maintenance

Risk Category	Guidance or discussion on mitigation
Poor quality software	ISE Library volume: *Improving the Maintainability of Software* Section 4.2.6
Ill-expressed requirement for change	Chapter 6 SSADM Version 4 Reference Manuals
Inadequate financial case	Chapter 6
Inadequate impact assessment	Chapter 6
Failure to change all relevant documentation when a change is made	Section 4.2.2
Resourcing, skill or motivation problems	Sections 6.8, 6.9
Insufficient standards or procedures	Chapters 5, 6
Inadequate change-control procedures	Chapter 6
Deadline pressures	Chapter 6
Insufficient test data	Chapter 7
Unrealistic expectations by customers	Section 4.2.3
Unrecognised need for preventive maintenance	Chapter 8

Figure 2: Guidance on the mitigation of maintenance risks

The remainder of section 4.2 highlights the most common risks associated specifically with software maintenance and offers advice on risk mitigation. Later chapters offer guidance on good practices that are relevant in the mitigation of maintenance risks, in relation to more generic IS management activities such as change management.

4.2.2 Change-documentation risks

Sometimes, it is difficult for managers to ensure that adequate time is taken for proper consideration of the implications of proposed software changes on the existing logical and physical designs of a system, bearing in mind the resource levels required. This is especially true where there are other considerations such as the original documentation standards or design methods not being those currently in use or familiar to maintenance staff.

Staff under pressure may perceive an easy, but flawed, solution without realising the full effect that the proposed change may have on the existing logical or physical design of the application system, or may fail to document changes properly.

It might appear that the assessment and correct documentation of changes is unproductive time when pressure is directed on finishing the task. However, it is essential that a full impact assessment of a proposed change is made at the start, and that changes are fully documented.

Both poor documentation and flawed solutions that take insufficient account of the design of the code affect the future maintainability of software, undermine the effect of using structured methods for development and hasten the need for the expensive option of carrying out a full redevelopment.

4.2.3 Risk of unrealistic customer expectations

Customer expectations are most effectively managed in an environment where there are laid-down policies and procedures covering maintenance and other requests for change. The users, business areas and maintainers should be involved in the process of handling requests for change, setting priorities and defining the implementation plan timescales. The assessment of each request for change should not only be done in terms of benefit and priority to the business, but should also take account of the full costs and the resource requirements to implement, install and use it. It is, of course, necessary to match activities against available resources. These processes and procedures are covered in detail in Chapter 6.

Chapter 4
Scope, risks and costs of maintenance

The implementation plan that is agreed by the users, business and maintainers should cover also the quality required of the changed software. Quality criteria to be used will vary from case to case. The stringency of the quality criteria depends on the criticality of the changed software to the business. Example criteria are that it must both support the new functionality required and the software is to be released only when there are no non-trivial known errors.

The lost value to the business, inherent in any backlog or delay, should influence the level of resources to be made available for maintenance activities.

4.2.4 Personal knowledge and staff-related risks

Often there is a grey area in assessments of proposed changes, in which decisions are based on personal knowledge of the maintainer as to when:

- relatively easy changes may be made to the software code of a system without going back to examine the original design in exhaustive detail

- a more rigourous approach is necessary because of an anticipated impact, going back to early stages of the original development processes to update the previous:
  - user requirement
  - requirements analysis and specification
  - technical system option
  - logical design
  - physical design

- consideration should be given to reverse engineering or redesigning and redeveloping the part of the application software in question, using current methods, tools and standards because:
  - the proposed change has such a radical impact on the existing code that if a cost benefit analysis is undertaken it is likely to

17

show one of these courses of action to be the best solution

- the system has become difficult to maintain as the original was poorly developed or subsequent maintenance has not followed the original logical and physical designs

- the obsolete skills and resources necessary to maintain the system, for example, language, development method or tools are becoming scarce or unavailable.

There are serious risks of the wrong decisions being made when:

- there is pressure due to management giving insufficient priority to the need to adequately assess any impact on the existing design

- the level of maintainers' knowledge is:
    - based purely on the code and not the design
    - based purely on the application software implementation and not the business need

- the motivation of maintenance personnel or the retention of high calibre maintenance personnel has not been a management priority.

Staff-related risks can be reduced by:

- adequately training and motivating personnel

- ensuring an appropriate skills and knowledge transfer between maintenance and development staff

- ensuring all future development and maintenance adheres to laid-down policies and procedures (see Chapter 5).

4.2.5 Risks associated with older systems

Risks increase where older systems:

- have been subject, at some point during original development or previous maintenance, to poor adherence to standards and procedures, particularly for documentation

- were not developed using current methods, standards or procedures

- where only a single individual, or a small number of people, have the necessary skills in the obsolete methods or tools used for earlier development or maintenance of the systems

- were produced in an obsolescent development environment and have not been brought up to date

- have test data that is inadequate or has not been adequately maintained for future regression testing.

4.2.6 Risk reduction through improved maintainability

Measures can be undertaken to reduce the risks associated with poor maintainability, for example:

- ensuring all new development and maintenance adheres to laid-down standards and policies, and in particular that it takes future maintenance into account

- carrying out preventive maintenance including reverse engineering.

Reverse engineering tools and techniques may be used to assist in:

- redocumenting inadequately documented systems

- restructuring poor code to:
  - accommodate future changes
  - improve readability
  - add explanatory comments
- measuring the complexity of code being managed
- redeveloping the code when it has become very difficult to maintain.

For further guidance on improving maintainability please refer to the Information Systems Engineering Library volume: *Improving the Maintainability of Software*.

4.3 Cost of maintenance

It is important that the IS customer and provider organisations understand and control the costs of software maintenance. To achieve this, they need to understand the cost of maintenance in each of the four categories. Resources expended on the implementation of changes in these four categories should be separately costed. Ongoing operational costs resulting from the changes should be similarly separated.

All perfective maintenance should be subject to a business case or investment appraisal. Ideally, the customer requiring the change should be required to pay for the work.

The costs of adaptive maintenance should be included in the investment appraisal for the changes in platform or environment. This investment may be a joint responsibility of the provider and the customer or may be shouldered by just one of the parties, depending on the nature and type of the change and the nature of the customer-provider relationship.

The costs of preventive maintenance should be subject to investment appraisal either from the provider's perspective of making IS provision more efficient and effective or from the customer's perspective of better quality, less costly IS changes. Input into this appraisal from any revision to the organisation's IS strategy and programme management may reflect likely new business needs and hence identify areas that are more likely to be subject to future change.

Corrective maintenance is usually the IS provider's responsibility and, in general, the cost has to be borne as an overhead. Corrective maintenance costs can be reduced by better quality of both development and testing of software. The increased development and testing costs that may be incurred to reduce the need for corrective maintenance should be assessed, not just against the cost of the corrective maintenance, but also against the potential cost to the business of IS failure.

Maintenance costs may be subject to resource ceilings and expenditure within and between categories decided on the basis of customer and, where appropriate, IS-provider priorities. However, both customer and IS-provider will require that:

- software faults, other than minor ones, must be fixed

- software changes to address new business requirements must be made

- obsolete hard-to-maintain software has to be replaced when it eventually becomes a liability

- new IT environments are needed from time to time.

Ongoing maintenance costs should be tracked and analysed. A high figure for corrective maintenance may indicate problems with the development process. A high figure for perfective maintenance may indicate a rapidly changing business or may be a warning that the customer community is not well-organised, and their expectations may need to be managed.

The historical costs of maintenance activity is often a good guide to predicting future costs. Proposed individual jobs can be compared to the cost and resources of similar completed jobs. Historical costs also show the overall accuracy of actual costs compared to the original estimates.

5 IS strategy and policies

5.1 IS strategy and software maintenance

An IS customer organisation's IS strategy sets out the organisation's intended future use of IS to meet the unfolding needs of the organisation's businesses. Figure 3 (overleaf) illustrates the IS lifecycle from business need through IS strategy to operational use. For simplicity the cyclic process of monitoring and replanning of IS exploitation is not shown. The shaded boxes show the place of software maintenance in relation to the organisation's IS strategy.

5.2 Maintenance portfolio

A portfolio of application system development or enhancement projects and of other software maintenance projects (such as for adaptive or preventive maintenance) are likely to be included in the strategy. This is explicitly shown in Figure 3 overleaf.

Small-scale perfective maintenance, those requests under the cost, size and risk limits set by the organisation, may be carried out as part of a business change programme required by the customer organisation or by some other arrangement. Such maintenance is subject of course to the usual rules of investment appraisal and the organisation's and IS provider's normal costing and charging rules. Typically, small changes are carried out under the organisation's ongoing change management procedures. They may be batched together with full project control arrangements invoked, if the scale or complexity of the changes makes that necessary. This type of change is shown in the Operational Running box in Figure 3.

The customer organisation's IS strategy is likely to make reference to major changes of IT infrastructure or to software platforms and environments. The need for such references is obvious in the case where the customer organisation wants to retain control over these items. In such circumstances the strategy should include a portfolio of adaptive maintenance projects.

Even if such major IT infrastructure changes are left to the provider, however, the customer organisation is likely to require notice and negotiations over such changes, as it may be impossible to make them without affecting the customer's IT services. The IS strategy would detail the requirements for notice and the negotiation period in respect of such changes. The strategy, therefore, generally infers the need for adaptive maintenance, other than where infrastructure or platform/environment changes do not require significant change to application software.

As an organisation's IS strategy unfolds, it may become clear that certain items of application software need to be redeveloped or rewritten. Preventive maintenance projects to deal with such situations should normally be referenced in the organisation's IS strategy, as indicated in Figure 3.

Corrective maintenance takes place as part of the organisation's normal ongoing problem management process (see Chapter 6), under full project control arrangements if the complexity or scale of the problem warrants it. This type of change is shown in the Operational Running box in Figure 3.

5.3 Management and technical policies

Software maintenance is a major issue that affects most IS customer and provider organisations. The customer organisation should have appropriate controls in place to help ensure that software maintenance contributes to the organisation's successful exploitation of IS, both at the time and into the future. Such controls are normally expressed as a set of management and technical policies that form part of the IS strategy. The IS provider may have its own policies, but these have to be compatible with those of the customer organisation.

Chapter 5
IS strategy and policies

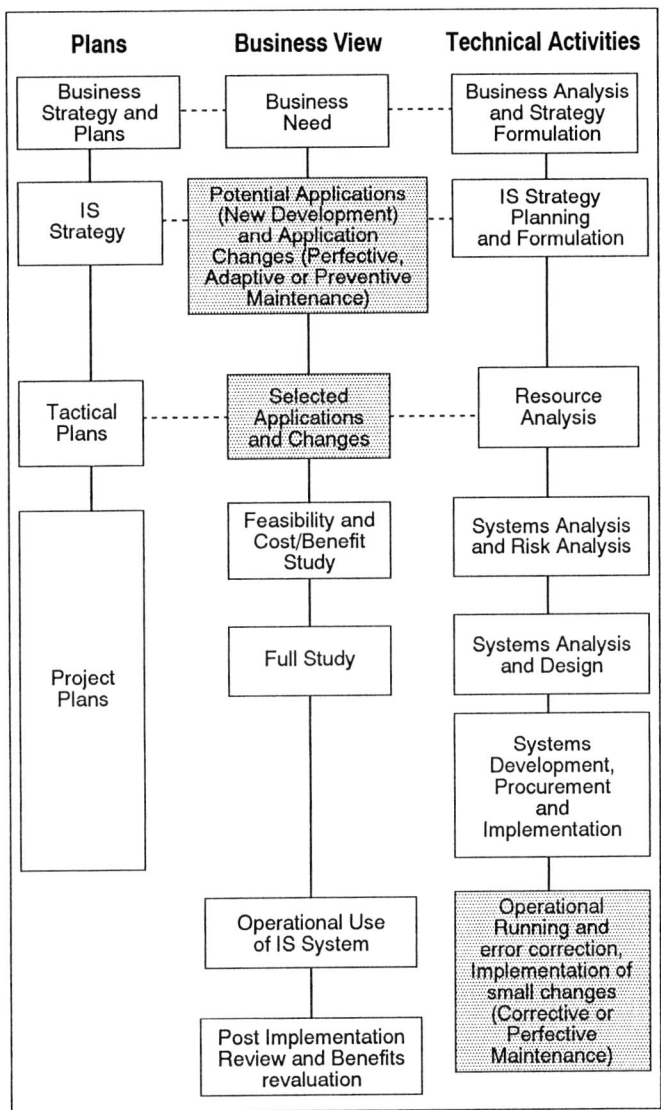

Figure 3: View of the parts of the IS lifecycle requiring policies for maintenance issues

Matters to be covered by software maintenance policies include:

- investment appraisal, costing and charging (see section 6.7). Note that it is very difficult to predict the costs of maintenance activity, especially corrective maintenance, which depends on the incidence and severity of errors. Historical costing data and, in some circumstances, techniques such as function point analysis can, however help. Further information on the use of function point analysis can be found in the Information Systems Engineering Library volume: *Estimating with Mark II Function Point Analysis*

- prioritisation and resourcing of maintenance activity. Often, these matters are largely subsumed within the organisation's problem management and change management systems (see section 6.1)

- change management. See Chapter 6 and the IT Infrastructure Library volume: *Change Management* for more information. Note that the policy should stipulate the circumstances in which a maintenance activity should be run under full project control, that is, when it is not small enough in cost, risk and resource terms to be run only under change management control

- problem management - see Chapter 6 and the IT Infrastructure Library volume: *Problem Management* for more information

- customer involvement in maintenance changes. Although subsumed in the organisation's other policies for maintenance, it may be useful to document this aspect of maintenance explicitly as a separate issue

- testing of maintenance changes (see Chapter 7)

- service level agreements covering maintenance. The time to effect corrective maintenance is covered by the organisation's problem management policies. The time to effect other types of maintenance should be covered by a specific maintenance project agreement, if it is not covered by the organisation's change management procedures. The cost of changes is covered by the organisation's costing and charging policies

- security issues, for example, security risk analysis and incident reporting

- quality requirements, for example, certification on the part of the maintainer under ISO 9001 or the TickIT scheme should be stated

- requirements for audits and reviews of the systems under maintenance, for management reports on these audits and reviews, and for follow-up action (see Chapter 8)

- requirements for reviews of the maintenance service itself (see Chapter 10)

- procedures, standards and methods to be used to ensure the customer organisation is not locked into proprietary services or products. For example, a requirement for SSADM documentation, the use of PRINCE for project control and to use CRAMM for security risk analysis during the system lifecycle, should be stated

- relation of software maintenance to software development and testing. That is, the need to track the frequency, importance, size and difficulty of corrective and adaptive maintenance changes, and take corrective action if there are indications of insufficient quality control in development and testing.

Similarly, it includes the need to track perfective maintenance to assess the volatility of customer requirements. A policy triggering preventive maintenance when appropriate should ease future maintenance and improve the quality of the software. Software development policies are needed to help ensure that easily maintainable systems are produced by the developers

- maintainers responsibility for conserving or improving maintainability. Further information can be found in the Information Systems Engineering Library volume: *Improving the Maintainability of Software*

- mechanisms for deciding when obsolescent software should be redeveloped or rewritten.

5.4 Special policies for old systems

Special policies may be needed for the maintenance of old application systems that were originally specified, developed or tested using procedures, methods or standards different from those that currently apply. For example, it would probably be unreasonable to group these systems together with those developed to current standards to derive unit costs for software maintenance overall. The use of separate figures for old software and software produced using current procedures, methods and standards would be preferable. Particularly where such software has been subject to frequent past modification, changes to old software are likely to take longer and cannot be expected to be as trouble free as changes to current software. There may, however, be some old software that is mature, stable and well understood, and consequently is relatively easy to maintain. The maintainability characteristics of the software should be reflected in the policies.

Chapter 5
IS strategy and policies

5.5 Original analysis, design, development and testing

The importance of software development and testing policies to the cost and quality of software maintenance cannot be overstated. The familiar maxim that fixing something that goes wrong at the design stage costs only £1, but that fixing a problem once the software is up and running costs over £1000, means that the quality of development and testing is extremely important. Use of structured design methods such as SSADM helps, as does the use of formal project management methods such as PRINCE. For further reading, please refer to the Information Systems Engineering Library volume: *Quality Management for PRINCE and SSADM Projects*, and the IT Infrastructure Library volume: *Testing an IT Service for Operational Use*.

5.6 Further advice

For further advice and guidance on this area, refer to the Information Systems Guide: *A2 Strategic Planning for Information Systems*. Detailed technical issues are covered in relevant volumes of the Information Systems Engineering Library: *Estimating with Mark II Function Point Analysis, Improving the Maintainability of Software* and *Quality Management for PRINCE and SSADM Projects* and the IT Infrastructure Library volumes: *Change Management, Problem Management* and *Testing an IT Service for Operational Use*.

Volumes in the IS Planning Subject Guides series are also likely to be of interest to readers.

6 Processes and organisation

6.1 Problem management

Much of the material in this chapter has been extracted from the IT Infrastructure Library. Further information is available in the volumes listed in Section 6.11. Software maintenance should be carried out under the control of the organisation's problem management and change management systems, as appropriate. These links are necessary to ensure the maintenance function does not adversely affect the quality of service delivered to the IS customers.

Problem management is necessary for corrective maintenance. After an incident has passed through the Help Desk and has been identified as a problem, it must be registered and assigned a priority depending on its severity. Once the error has been corrected, the software must be tested and, when these tests have been completed satisfactorily, the amended software may be brought into use via release control procedures. Emergency changes are covered in Section 6.5. Errors requiring very significant change may need to be handled as a project under full Change Management control.

The software maintenance providers should furnish one or more of the specialist teams that support the problem management function.

Problem management statistics show the incidence and any rate of change of the incidence of errors across the organisation's software base. This information should be used to:

- reduce the error rate through preventive maintenance and the adoption of problem management principles, especially in respect of more serious errors

- identify items of software that are unreliable and may need extensive remedial work or rewrite

- ascertain whether there are problems affecting the software development area that are having an adverse effect on operational software and, if so, take remedial action.

The control and review of software systems is covered in more detail in Chapter 8.

6.2 Change management

Full change management procedures apply to all forms of maintenance other than corrective. Large scale changes must be authorised by the Change Advisory Board and handled as major projects and their deliverables must be subject to target dates. Functionality and quality agreements must be drawn up between IS provider and customer. The impact of such large changes on other parts of the organisation and on the IT infrastructure need to be taken into account and addressed at the project initiation stage. A priority should be assigned to the change which reflects the organisation's business needs and a cost/benefit assessment.

Smaller scale changes should be subjected to the disciplines of the change management system. Each change should be assigned a priority for attention. Authorisation for the work to proceed should be given by the Change Manager only after there has been an impact assessment and a target date for the completion of the change, including testing.

Changes are authorised by the Change Manager who acts on advice from the Change Advisory Board. The Change Advisory Board has representatives from business, user and IS provider interests.

The change management system helps to ensure that only changes that are mandatory or of value to the organisation are carried out, and that changes are implemented in a controlled manner. Requests for change are normally raised by IS customers in response to a change in their perceived needs, or occasionally by the IS provider. In general, those who benefit from the change should pay for the implementation of the change and its ongoing cost.

The software maintenance function should have representation on the Change Advisory Board. Software maintenance staff provide essential information concerning the cost, practicability, timescale and impact of requested changes to software. The detection of knock-on impact is an important feature of the input from software maintenance. This impact would include identifying where:

- a change affects software used elsewhere

- a requested change to one service requires changes to other services

- a requested non-IT change requires consequent IT changes and vice versa.

6.3 Configuration management

All error correction and change activity on software must be recorded and co-ordinated. The use of a configuration management system can provide automated help to software maintainers and to the change management function. It can also assist with providing impact assessments.

6.4 Change control procedures

It is inappropriate, in this volume, to describe the likely content of an organisation's change control procedures in detail, but they must include provision for:

- a clear, well understood process for approval or rejection of a change request on the grounds of business needs. The process should include the taking of advice on requested changes from the business or policy area, the users of the application system and the IS providers

- the specification and justification of the user requirement for each change

- an estimate of the saving/benefit to the business which would follow the successful implementation of the change

- an assessment of the consequential impact on technical plans, for example, security, maintainability and quality plans

- estimates of the time and cost of implementation where the work:

    - is an individual project

    - could wait to be incorporated with other agreed amendments, perhaps of a different priority, to the same part of the system to reduce costs overall

- an opportunity for those who may be affected by the change to make comments on the proposed change, for example, recipients of output from the system.

Further detailed information can be found in the IT Infrastructure Library volume: *Change Management*.

If effective procedures are not in place or are not followed, there is a serious risk that work may not be correctly evaluated or given the right priority. This may lead to effort being expended on low priority amendments, while essential changes are not implemented on time with possible serious consequences for the business.

6.5 Emergency changes

There is need for urgent change procedures to cater for emergency error corrections or imposed changes in business practice. However, all possible attempts should be made to accommodate the normal full levels of analysis, design and testing within the limits of practicality. Emergency changes should be regarded as only temporary and should be followed up by a change following the standard change management process. This follow-up action enables the support staff to evaluate the hastily made changes and, if necessary, implement a more satisfactory and properly tested amendment to preserve the integrity of the logical and physical structure of the system.

Chapter 6
Processes and organisation

6.6 **Release control**

Establishing a procedure for the release control of software is recommended. The aim is to have a planned, published and agreed programme for releases of updated software showing the target date for, and the changes to be included in, each release. This arrangement facilitates forward planning by the IS providers as well as the customer. Experience has shown that without a plan of this kind, the customer is unaware of implementation dates, leading to confusion and misunderstanding including, for example, allocating insufficient time for a user retraining programme.

The time interval between releases and the extent of amendments incorporated in each need to be arranged to meet specific needs. Releases that are either too frequent or incorporate too much change are likely to cause reliability problems and can be disruptive to the customers. The statistics from the change management and control processes show the rate of change requests and the priority of the changes affecting the various items in the organisation's software base. This information should be used to identify:

- areas where there is a high volatility of customer requirements which may lead to the need to manage customer expectations

- items of software that may need to be restructured or partly rewritten in future preventive maintenance

- problems in the software development area in which case remedial action should be instigated.

6.7 **Post implementation review**

Changes or corrections introduced as a result of software maintenance should be subject to a review at some time, typically a few weeks after implementation. The objective of the review is to determine whether:

- the change or correction worked as expected
- the cost of the change was as expected

- the expected benefits to the business are being or can be realised

- there are any lessons to learn for future maintenance activities (this is often determined separately by an earlier project evaluation review).

This review is in addition to the normal testing and monitoring of changes and corrections by the operational service providers. The review should in general be carried out by representatives of the business, user and IS provider areas.

Where maintenance projects are carried out as part of an IS related programme, the post implementation review (PIR) of a maintenance change would contribute to the PIR for the programme. The programme PIR is concerned primarily with reviewing the benefits realisation. Programme PIR are carried out not just once but from time to time after programme implementation.

6.8 Prioritisation of maintenance activity

In most circumstances, it is not possible to implement all the requests for change or to deal with all problems within the required timescale that customers might desire. For change requests, it is necessary to have a clear mechanism and policy for assessing and occasionally escalating priorities and a Change Advisory Board to help the Change Manager to manage the process. This approach ensures that the most important work is completed on time without losing sight of less urgent tasks.

It is essential that the prioritisation of changes takes account of the needs of business customers, application users and IS providers. All these functions should be represented on the Change Advisory Board.

Any mandatory changes, such as those required to comply with changes in legislation, clearly have to be dealt with to a set deadline. Other changes have to be prioritised and any deadlines calculated on their merits, having regard to:

- the cost and benefit of the change
- the cost and other consequences of not implementing the change
- the impact on customer satisfaction levels, particularly for long outstanding items
- the availability of resources to carry out the work.

Care must be taken to ensure that low priority changes are not ignored. Periodically, the backlog of change requests needs to be reviewed. Long outstanding items may need to be reprioritised, regrouped differently with other changes, rescheduled or deleted.

Similar considerations apply to the correction of errors. The priority for resources to put things right should be based upon the severity of the error. This does not mean that all errors of the same severity can be corrected equally quickly as some will be more difficult to resolve than others.

6.9 Allocation of appropriate resources

The organisation's management needs to be aware of the extent of any backlog of maintenance work and the consequences to the business of the non-implementation of requested changes or the non-correction of errors. The aim is to ensure that there are sufficient resources available to carry out all the work required to maintain the functionality and quality of each system being maintained.

Following periodic reviews of the application systems, it may be appropriate to allocate more resources to the maintenance area to enable vital work to be carried out on systems which support important business applications.

Although experienced software maintenance personnel are expensive, this resource cost must be measured against possible savings to the business stemming from the removal of the maintenance backlog and against the overall quality of the service provided to the organisation's customers. It can be argued that there is a case for putting the most experienced and skilled staff on maintenance tasks. Maintenance is a more complex task that development, since the maintainer has to acquire an understanding of the existing system before designing any changes to it.

Conversely, a review of outstanding maintenance work and its priority may indicate that some maintenance staff may be moved to different activities or projects.

6.10 **Organisation of a maintenance unit**

The organisation of application development and maintenance staff and the allocation of work between them can have an impact on productivity and the quality of the work carried out. The aim is to minimise the risk of conflicting responsibilities, conflicting timescales and the mixed use of both current and superseded techniques and standards, which can cause unnecessary stress and ultimately lead to mistakes being made.

As far as possible, software maintenance work should be separated from development work and, within maintenance, it is desirable to distinguish between perfective and other categories of maintenance.

The principal difference between development and all categories of software maintenance work is that development often has longer timescales and involves the generation of entirely new facilities, whereas maintenance involves understanding an existing system to identify where required changes need to be made, often in limited timescales.

Perfective maintenance sits in a grey area with aspects of the work resembling development and aspects resembling other categories of maintenance. It often calls for similar skills to development work, but with the added complexity of having to integrate entirely new or revised features with existing processes without degrading the logical and physical design of the whole of the existing system.

Corrective maintenance typically requires a rapid response to rectify a fault in the application system which may be preventing the processing of vital data. Some people find this type of work less stimulating and less creative than new development or perfective maintenance.

Although the boundaries between these different categories of work are not clear cut, efforts should be made to ensure that any individual is only engaged on one type of activity at a time. This enables staff to concentrate on the specific skills needed for a given task, avoids confusion and conflicting pressures and contributes to meeting required deadlines.

Software maintenance can be an important contributor to the provision of successful IS support to the IS provider's customers. Staff should be encouraged to view the work in that way.

6.11 Further advice

Further detailed advice and guidance on this area can be found in the IT Infrastructure Library Service Support Set, particularly the volumes: *Change Management, Configuration Management, Help Desk, Problem Management* and *Software Control and Distribution*.

7 Testing

7.1 Development practices

All perfective software maintenance arises because the software does not have all the functionality required by the customer. It is, therefore, important that software developers understand what customers want and liaise with them at all stages of software development to help ensure their requirements are met.

Use of a structured method discipline during development and coding will help to minimise the introduction of errors during the development stage, that test cases can be simplified and that those errors which do arise are quickly corrected.

However, in software development it is impossible to eliminate all development errors every time. The developed software must be properly tested. Similar requirements apply to software that is corrected or amended as a result of any software maintenance.

7.2 Amendment testing

Testing can never fully prove the correctness of an information system. However, well designed test cases can identify most errors. Failure to carry out adequate testing leads to:

- the increased risk of run-time errors or system failure

- the need for additional corrective maintenance, with consequent cost and disruption to planned schedules of work

- a greater risk of security problems

- incorrect processing of data and possible serious consequences for the business.

Great care should therefore be taken in developing suitable test cases for each component of a system and for the system as a whole.

It is essential that all new or changed code should be properly tested before being incorporated into a live system. The necessary tests should be set out as part of the specification of the user requirement for each change request, with test cases produced and agreed between the customers and the IS providers. As a minimum standard, test cases should be prepared to ensure that each procedural line of code written for, or directly affected by, an amendment is activated at least once.

The aim is to take all reasonable steps to ensure that changes to existing systems are made correctly in accordance with the customer requirement.

7.3 **Regression testing**

Even though the code written to implement a change may appear to be error free, there is always the risk that the introduction of the change may cause incorrect processing of data elsewhere in the organisation's software. The aim of regression testing is to carry out controlled tests on the whole portfolio of software that could conceivably be affected by the change, using existing proven test cases. This should increase confidence that the impact analysis was correct and that the current change has not interfered with the processing of unchanged software.

An appropriate set of test cases must be retained and itself properly maintained for regression testing. It is necessary to modify these test cases to keep them aligned with the changes made. Great care must always be taken to preserve the appropriateness and correctness of the test cases for future use.

7.4 **Risks associated with limited testing**

Full regression testing of all the software that might be affected should be the default for all new releases of software, whether the release is to introduce enhancements or to correct errors. Sometimes, however, the constraint of pressing deadlines, limited resources or the nature of the software or the change may tempt implementers to limit testing to save time and cost.

Chapter 7
Testing

It is essential that all those concerned with the development, modification or acceptance of software recognise the potentially serious risks involved in allowing limited testing. Clear guidelines should be established for assessing the increased risk of failure from reducing the scope of software testing, against the apparent benefit of speeding up the implementation of a change. The aim of such guidelines is to provide a standard means against which a decision on the required rigour of testing can be made. For example, there is little risk from a change that corrects the text of a rarely-used output message. There is a high risk from a change that attempts to correct an error resulting from a design fault in software code that modifies an important piece of business information in a live database. In the latter case, extensive testing is needed.

Potential problems occur when changes are made to software code that:

- accesses live data

- is frequently used

- calls on or interacts with other sections of software code

- is invoked from other items of software.

or when changes themselves:

- are large or complex

- affect the design of the software

- involve complex software coding

- involve software that is critically important to business operations or business success

- impact on the integrity and functionality of system's sccurity features

- reflect non-trivial changes in the user requirement

- are to correct high-severity errors.

In the case of error corrections, a compromise may need to be made between the requirements for urgent rectification and the requirement not to introduce or reintroduce other problems. Maintaining a distinction between incident handling, restoring the service, and problem handling, correcting the underlying cause of failure, can help. The latter clearly has to be done well, whereas the most important considerations for a temporary fix may be to get part of the system restored and not to introduce further faults. Even so, care should be taken not to add unjustifiable risks by inadequate testing.

Where different degrees of thoroughness of regression testing may be appropriate for a given item of software, two or more sets of test cases may be prepared providing predetermined levels of testing. The circumstances in which each level of testing should be used must be clearly stated and agreed.

Any decision to limit testing, due to shortage of time, should be taken only with the prior agreement of the business managers, the application users and the IS maintainers. In arriving at a decision, those responsible should pay full attention to the possible consequences of incorrect processing of live data and the added risks, costs and inconvenience of having to make an emergency correction to the system.

Where testing has been limited, there is no reason to stop testing when a change goes live. It is still worth testing to try to find errors before they occur in the live environment, as the cost is purely that of the correction and the greater cost of repairing and restoring a failed live system and data may be saved.

Chapter 7
Testing

7.5 Sign off

Once the maintainers have coded an agreed change or corrected an error and completed their own tests, the application users should be involved in the amendment and regression testing described above.

The aim is to ensure that the customer requirement is fully met and to provide both business managers and application users with confidence in the reliability and usability of the amended software.

When the customers and operational service providers are satisfied that the system is functioning correctly, the release should be signed off by the business manager and IT service manager. The amended software then becomes subject to the normal release control procedures for live running.

7.6 Further advice

Further advice on all aspects of release control and software testing can be obtained from the IT Infrastructure Library volumes: *Software Control and Distribution*, *Software Lifecycle Support* and *Testing an IT Service for Operational Use*.

Management of Software Maintenance

8 Control and review of software systems

8.1 Need for reviews

Adopting the guidance in earlier chapters should reduce the risk of software failure and contribute to the quality of software. Nevertheless, it is important to review the current state of application systems from time to time to detect any trends in maintenance activity on the systems and to monitor their overall condition. Data from the organisation's change management and problem management systems may provide much of the information needed to carry out such reviews.

The aim is to obtain early warning of any deterioration in an application system which would affect its quality, reliability or maintainability, for example, changes becoming both more difficult to implement and followed by an increasing error rate. The availability of such indications for all the software being maintained enables the IS provider to decide whether and where additional effort should be expended to improve the quality and reliability of systems, thus increasing their value to the organisation. Deploying resources where they are most needed greatly increases the effectiveness and efficiency of the software maintenance area.

The following paragraphs provide an overview of the routine actions which need to be taken to make informed decisions possible.

8.2 Activity measurement

To monitor the organisation's application software and to control maintenance activity on it, it is necessary to keep good records of the nature and extent of the maintenance activity undertaken. An important aim is to have up-to-date reliable information on all the application systems being maintained to facilitate meaningful system audits, as outlined in section 8.3 below.

Therefore, it is recommended that a formal record of perfective and corrective maintenance be kept for each application showing:

- mandatory changes and their priority

- requests for desirable change and their priority

- errors reported and their severity

- for each of the above, a record of the resources used to implement each change, and of the time taken between:

    - initial notification of the need for action

    - agreement to proceed

    - implementation of the change or correction

    - also, a record of any quality problems and of resources and timings for any necessary rework.

Any activity on adaptive and preventive maintenance should be similarly recorded.

8.3 System audits

Using the above information in conjunction with maintainers' and customers' views on the current state of the software, and data on the extent of any backlog of change requests and uncorrected errors, a periodic audit of each application system should be carried out. This audit should be done at least annually and show:

- the total maintenance effort spent, subdivided by each of the four categories of maintenance

- any rate of change in maintenance requests over the period

- the degree of backlog, the outstanding costs to clear the backlog, the lost benefit as a result of the backlog, the estimated total and average time to clear, and whether deadlines are being met for both:

    - change requests

    - errors to be corrected

Chapter 8
Control and review of software systems

- the degree of customer satisfaction with:
  - each existing system as it stands
  - the level of maintenance service.

The aim is to obtain a snapshot of each application system for comparison with other systems at the same time and for comparison with the same application system over a period of time.

System audits provide a simple but powerful approach for the IS provider to monitor any changes in the apparent maintainability of each system in its control.

8.4 Control actions

Having carried out an audit on each application system, there should be a full review of all the applications being maintained involving the business managers, the application users and the IS providers.

The aim is to note any trends or changes that have occurred since the last review and to decide what action should be taken to halt or reverse any deterioration in application system quality or in the quality of support to the business applications.

Resources can then be directed to the most important applications or problem areas ensuring that the maintainers concentrate on those tasks that have been given a high priority by the users and business managers.

The nature of any control actions depends on the results of the review and the availability of resources. Apart from reallocation of resources from one application system to another, or among the different types of maintenance, or possibly between development and maintenance, it may be necessary to carry out remedial action on particular items of software.

Separately, or in combination, the following remedial actions would prove beneficial in appropriate circumstances:

- restructure all or part of a system

- rewrite key programs which may have become difficult to amend, to reflect changed business requirements

- reverse engineer a system to bring it into line with the policies and methods that apply currently to new software developments in the organisation, for example, documentation standards or analysis and design methods such as SSADM

- obtain software tools to facilitate analysis of code or monitoring of automated program testing.

There comes a time when it is clear that a system is no longer appropriate to the present business of the organisation or it has decayed beyond the point where reasonable remedial action would be cost effective. In such circumstances, a new system needs to be developed in order to provide the functionality and quality of service required. Early warning of the inadequacy of an existing system is provided through the regular audit and review processes for maintenance work.

Signs to look for include:

- when changes to the functionality of the system cannot be incorporated

- when changes which can be made are regularly taking longer than originally judged reasonable to implement

- when there is an increasing frequency of runtime errors, especially following new releases of the software

- when the cost of maintaining and running the system is approaching the value of the system to the business.

Chapter 8
Control and review of software systems

8.5 Feedback to software developers

An additional benefit of audit and review of systems under maintenance is that lessons can be learnt concerning how to develop new systems which are easier to maintain. Feeding such information back to those engaged in the development of new systems reduces maintenance difficulties in the future.

9 Contracting out software maintenance

9.1 Issues and risks

9.1.1 Existing issues and risks

All the existing issues and risks attendant on managing software maintenance in-house apply equally when maintenance is contracted out. Some difficulties may be regarded as being eased, perhaps owing to the commercial arrangement or the contractor's specialisations, or heightened, because of the organisation's concern over loss of direct control or the contractor's inexperience of the organisation's business and IS. In addition, some further issues and risks outlined in the rest of this chapter need to be addressed and resolved as and when appropriate.

9.1.2 Reasons for consideration

There are a number of reasons for considering the use of an external contractor to meet some or all of an organisation's software maintenance needs. For example:

- government policy requires government organisations to undertake market testing for the provision of services. Software maintenance might be chosen as a potential candidate for testing to ensure that services are delivered at best value for money

- there may be a requirement to release staff for other work. For example, those with particular knowledge of the business requirement or a present application may be needed to develop a replacement system

- the essential staff skills for maintaining a particular system are no longer available

- there may be inadequate staff resources to cope with the current demand

- there may be a lack of confidence in the internal organisation to meet targets

9.1.3 Management issues and risks

Issues and risks primarily related to the management of the organisation's relationship with an external contracted maintainer are that:

- the service level specification and change control procedures embodied in the contract are formal. These may prove inflexible in the light of changing business requirements unless they are carefully designed to cater for all possible events, for example:

    - legislation or government policy mandating changes at short notice

    - an unexpected extension to, or contraction of, the life of an application

    - the need for changed response or performance levels on the part of the maintainer during the period of the contract

- there is a danger of lock-in to a particular contractor or to proprietary products or tools used by the contractor. This may be reduced if it is addressed in the contract by ensuring that non-proprietary methods, agreed tools and appropriate standards are used and that adequate control and sufficient technical expertise are retained in the organisation's own Service Control Team (SCT) to manage the contract

- it may be difficult to ensure the contractor adheres to the organisation's IS policies, for example, its security policy. This problem may be alleviated by stating a requirement for quality audits in the contract

- there may be difficulties of hand-over to a different contractor or hand back at the end of a contract. This problem may be reduced if it is planned for with the appropriate procedures laid down in the contract

Chapter 9
Contracting out software maintenance

- it may be hard to effect a speedy recovery of assets, for example, systems, software tools, data and up-to-date documentation, if the contractor unexpectedly ceases trading

- it is difficult to estimate the cost of maintenance services because the amount of maintenance activity is not always predictable. Equally, it is difficult to assess the reasonableness of charges levied on a time and materials basis because of the difficulty in estimating the resource required to effect particular maintenance changes. Use of techniques such as Function Point Analysis may help

- there are liaison, communication and boundary issues between the contractors' staff, the SCT, application developers and the IS customer managers. These need to be carefully managed to avoid difficulties, particularly if other services are contracted out, or more than one contractor is involved.

9.1.4 Scope of contracting out for software maintenance

The scope of a contract for external maintenance services can be:

- limited to purely corrective maintenance, for example, dealing with bugs solely to keep an existing system running unchanged until a planned termination or replacement

- limited to adaptive and corrective maintenance, for example, to port an application to a different system environment and to rectify any known bugs at the same time

- the full range of corrective, adaptive, perfective and preventive maintenance

- limited to a particular hardware platform or applications written in a particular language, for example, to overcome a skills shortage

- limited to a particular business function or area

- part of a traditional turnkey solution to provide both the original development and ongoing maintenance

- part of a wider facilities management (FM) scheme to contract out more than just software maintenance activities.

9.1.5 Duration of contract

The period for which external support for software maintenance may be considered could be:

- short term, to carry out preventive maintenance and thereby improve the maintainability of a system for the future

- short term, for example, a conversion exercise from a particular proprietary system environment

- medium term, for example, to maintain a particular application system until it is replaced or until a planned cessation of use

- longer term, for example, to maintain application systems externally on a permanent basis.

In any event, the contract should be for a finite period with the expectation that a rebidding exercise will be required at the end of the period and with arrangements made to ensure that a smooth handover can be made at that stage to another party, if appropriate.

9.1.6 Staffing issues and risks

Issues and risks primarily related to staffing matters include:

- the introduction of third party support and the possible need to second or transfer some members of staff with a knowledge of the application to the contractor. This situation needs to be handled tactfully and using appropriate staff transfer conditions

- the difficulty of retaining in the organisation an adequate knowledge of the application from

Chapter 9
Contracting out software maintenance

business and technical perspectives. This problem can be addressed by ensuring that there is an adequately staffed SCT with sufficient technical expertise to manage the contract and act as the intelligent customer for the maintenance service, on behalf of the business users of the maintained applications.

9.1.7 Technical issues and risks

Issues and risks primarily related to technical matters may concern:

- knowledge transfer considerations, for example:

    - lack of background knowledge on the part of the maintainer of how the business operates. The contractor should be briefed and should be able to demonstrate an understanding of the business before the contract is awarded

    - difficulties likely to be experienced by the maintainer in obtaining detailed knowledge of the application and its code especially if it is poorly documented. The contractor must be able to demonstrate an ability to acquire this knowledge rapidly, for example, using reverse engineering tools to generate documentation from the software code

    - a possible lack of knowledge or skills in the methodologies used to develop the application by the maintainer. The skill levels required by third party staff should have been evaluated during the contractor selection exercise, and can also be specified in the contract, for example, ISEB certificate in IT infrastructure management or SSADM V4 certificate of proficiency

- consideration of overall quality of service. Evaluation of the contractors at the selection stage may, for example, take account of whether a contractor is certified under ISO 9001 or the TickIT scheme. The SCT should monitor the overall quality of service

- a requirement to adhere to the technical standards and methods laid down in the organisation's IS policies and a requirement to ensure the quality of third party work and adherence to testing and other working procedures. These requirements can be addressed by specifying an ongoing audit by the SCT.

9.2 Benefits

The principal benefits stemming from the contracting out of maintenance services are likely to be:

- that contracting out may offer improved effectiveness and value for money when compared to the internal service

- that the day-to-day management of maintenance projects and activities is limited to the overall specification and control of the maintenance service and to the specification and monitoring of specific maintenance projects and changes

- that the third party may be able to allocate additional staff resources to cater for peaks in the workload

- that cost benefit analyses for possible enhancements can be firmly based on contractual quoted costs as opposed to estimates, to balance against firmly costed business benefits.

Contracting out may be the correct outcome if a market testing exercise shows that this offers the service required together with the best overall value for money.

9.3 Further advice

Chapter 10 gives an outline step-by-step approach to the specification, agreement and monitoring of a software maintenance service that is to be run at arm's length from the customer, by a contractor or an in-house provider.

Further detailed advice and guidance on contracting out and on the provision of service at arm's length can be found in the Information Systems Guides: *A2 Strategic Planning for Information Systems* and *E4 Facilities Management*, and in the IT Infrastructure Library: *Managing Facilities Management, Managing Supplier Relationships, Service Level Management* and *Third Party and Single Source Maintenance*.

In addition, CCTA has produced a set of market testing IS/IT booklets and management briefings.

10 Software maintenance services at arm's length

10.1 Provision of services at arm's length

Chapter 9 covered the issues, risks and benefits associated with the contracting out of software maintenance services.

There is a growing trend towards having an arm's length relationship between the customer organisation's business areas and the maintainers irrespective of whether software maintenance is provided by contractors or from within the customer organisation, for example, by an in-house IT Directorate. This is a trend that is also affecting the arrangements for other IS provision services such as software development and operational service provision. The trend has its origins in the drive towards greater accountability by service providers for the quality and cost of their services. The onus is on the customer areas to clearly specify their requirements.

In such an arm's length arrangement, the expectations that the customer and provider have of the service are documented in a service agreement. When customer and provider are in different organisations the service agreement forms part of a contract between the two parties.

10.2 Statement of service requirement

As a first step towards the setting up of a service agreement, the customer organisation has to define its requirements for a maintenance service. The business areas are likely to need help from the IS advisors in their Service Control Team (SCT) to define their requirements. The SCT will also manage the relationship with the service provider. Where market testing is being carried out the SCT IS advisors form part of the intelligent customer function described in the CCTA market testing publications. The customer's service requirements are documented in a Statement of Service Requirement (SSR).

The SSR can be used under formal procurement rules to invite competitive bids for the provision of the service. In the remainder of this chapter, it is assumed that the maintenance service is obtained by means of a competitive procurement as part of a market testing exercise. For guidance on the procurement process please refer to the CCTA publication: *A Guide to Procurement within the Total Acquisition Process* (TAP). This guide explains when it is necessary to advertise in the Official Journal of the European Communities prior to issuing an SSR.

Parts of the SSR may indicate issues on which agreement has to be reached between the customer and provider before the service starts. The rest of the SSR states requirements of the service that are already defined.

Items to be covered in the SSR include:

- the service itself
- contract management arrangements
- policies and standards
- service monitoring and auditing
- termination and hand-over
- additional demands on the providers.

Each of these is covered in more detail below.

10.2.1 The service

The service itself includes:

- the nature of the service to be provided, for example, corrective and perfective maintenance and any additional services such as customer support
- the location of the service
- the strategic framework within which the service is to operate, for example, under the control of the customer's IS strategy

- any contractual commitments, licensing arrangements, third party agreements, warranties and liabilities associated with the software, the hardware upon which it runs, and the systems with which it interfaces. Later agreement and negotiation will be needed on issues such as the maintainer's responsibilities and rights in respect of any licensing conditions applying to relevant items of software

- the service IT environment which includes:
    - the software to be covered by the service. This requires a complete list and description of the application systems, their functions, the operational service supported and the customer needs met by the systems
    - the computer system platforms used
    - the age and size of the application systems
    - any statistics on current and past maintenance activity on the application, also statistics pertaining to the maintainability of the applications

- the customer base for the service and any projected changes to the customer base

- the portfolio of maintenance and enhancement projects currently defined in the organisation's project portfolio

- the quality criteria that must be adhered to for the maintenance service as a whole. Matters to be covered might include:
    - time to implement corrections, by error severity, or to notify customers of reasons for delay and agree steps to be taken to complete the work. Note that the time required depends on the complexity of the problem

- time to implement changes, by priority. Note that this time depends on the complexity and size of the change

- rules to be applied to decide whether an implemented change or correction is satisfactory

• any security requirements relating to the confidentiality, integrity and availability of information and related IS/IT assets

• the interfaces with and dependencies on, other services

• the volume of maintenance work in terms of the number and size of changes and corrections. If possible, expected maximum and minimum volumes should be given. For example, it is expected that there will be between 200 and 400 software errors of average complexity to be corrected per annum. However, if the volume falls below 150 or rises above 450, then contract change control procedures (see below) are to be invoked.

10.2.2 Contract management

Contract management arrangements cover:

• any rules to be applied in respect of individual maintenance projects or changes, as and when these occur, to agree the timescales, costs and other quality criteria that are to govern the maintenance activity. Any other rules or procedures pertaining to the take on of new maintenance work. Negotiation on these matters will be needed before a service agreement can be finalised

• the arrangements to be applied for the acceptance into the service agreement of new software by the maintainer

Chapter 10
Software maintenance services at arm's length

- a requirement to define rules and arrangements for billing or charging, for example, if the customer requires statistics or other information to substantiate the provider's charges this should be stated. The customer is likely to require a statement of the provider's charging formulae. In addition agreement will be needed on the rules to be applied in respect of tariff variations. Agreement will be needed on any minimum charges, in case volumes fall below expected levels

- the need to define change control arrangements for the contract, in particular authorisation procedures and costing/charging arrangements when the service agreement is modified or the workload is changed

- the need to agree other contract management procedures such as dispute resolution procedures.

10.2.3 Policies and standards

Policies and standards include:

- policies and standards to be applied to the service, for example, adherence to the organisation's change and problem management systems and the use of SSADM for perfective, corrective and preventive maintenance

- any requirements for the maintainer to be certified to the international quality standard ISO9001, plus any additional requirements for agreement on the provider's processes, to give the customer confidence that required services will be provided at low risk.

10.2.4 Service monitoring

Service monitoring and auditing covers:

- arrangements for monitoring the services, reviewing the provider's performance and agreeing follow-up actions, any arrangements for monitoring customer satisfaction with the services

- the need to define arrangements for auditing of software and the follow-up actions

- any requirements for quality audits of the provider's activities and the follow-up actions

- arrangements for forward planning of the services, in particular the customer's responsibility for providing information on future requirements for software changes as these become known.

10.2.5 Termination and handover

Termination and hand-over includes:

- the duration of the requirement and the need to agree termination criteria and arrangements including the period of notice pertaining to either party

- the need to agree handover arrangements for the start and the end of the contract

- the need to agree arrangements for bidders to assess the state of software to be maintained.

10.2.6 Additional demands

Additional demands on the providers contains:

- any flexibilities required of the maintenance personnel being bought-in as part of the service, for example, their use on other tasks in slack periods

- any requirements for the maintainer to assess, report on and improve on the maintainability of software

- any responsibility of the provider to be proactive in suggesting ways of improving the services.

Any other information that may be relevant to bidders, such as a plan to replace a mainframe computer system in two years time, should be stated in the SSR.

In drawing up the SSR the customer organisation should be aware of the funds available for spending on the service. This information should not be released to bidders who will be judged on the basis of their charges and the quality of service that they offer. As previously indicated, it is difficult for customer organisations to assess the right level of charges for maintenance services: the amount of maintenance likely to be needed is hard to predict and the amount of work that should be involved in carrying it out is hard to judge. Past experience of the organisation's existing software base or comparisons with other organisations' software bases may be helpful, but is not entirely reliable. Expert assistance may be needed.

Once the SSR has been completed, proposed draft contracts are drawn up and issued with the SSR to potential providers, as described in the CCTA TAP guidance. The proposals received in response to the SSR are then evaluated and a shortlist is drawn up.

10.3 Service agreement

Discussions take place with shortlisted providers to clarify outstanding points and negotiate draft contracts. Best and final offers are sought and a contract is awarded to the organisation that offers the required, or better, services at the most cost effective price. The contract embodies not only the service agreement, but also includes, for example, a description of the service and agreed charges.

When the chosen provider is an in-house organisation, or when the provider is part of another Crown organisation, a contract is not appropriate but a service agreement is still drawn up.

The contract or service agreement documents the customer's and provider's expectations of the services to be provided as follows:

- the specification of the services

- the responsibility of both parties

- the arrangements governing the relationship between the two sides including the way in which service performance will be measured

- the policies that are to apply to the provided services.

All arrangements for which a need is expressed in the SSR should be documented.

10.4 Service monitoring

The service provided must be monitored by the customer in relation to the requirements in the contract or service agreement, and should be reviewed from time to time with the provider. The items to be monitored and the frequency of monitoring are defined in the agreement.

10.4.1 Monthly monitoring

Typically the following will be checked monthly:

- service quality

- charges

- the state of software systems

- any backlogs.

The maintenance requirements for the next few months should be reviewed at the same time and arrangements drawn up for the maintainer to take on the new work. If there were any significant problems, a rectification plan will be agreed. Progress on actions from the previous review should be monitored.

10.4.2 Quarterly monitoring

On a quarterly basis additional checks may be made on:

- customer satisfaction
- adherence to policies and standards
- the maintainability of software
- any requirements to amend the service agreement.

A plan for the following six months' service would be agreed in outline.

10.4.3 Annual monitoring

Annually a full quality audit may be carried out depending on the requirement embodied in the contract or service agreement. The requirements could be as follows:

- an audit of the provider's ISO9001 certification by the registering body
- assessment of the provider's effectiveness at meeting the the customer's requirements and the charges levied on the provider
- identifying proposed changes to IS strategy as a result of monitoring the service
- to inform the provider of IS strategy changes relevant to the maintenance service
- agree an outline plan of the next 18 months
- reach agreement on plans to amend the contract or service agreement.

The customer could at this time give notice of any intention to terminate the service or to carry out a new competition by means of an advertisement in the Official Journal of the European Communities. It would be open for the provider to rebid.

Bibliography

Information Systems Guides

The Information Systems Guides, are available from John Wiley & Sons Ltd, Baffins Lane, Chichester PO19 1UD.

The following guides are referenced in this publication:

- CCTA IS Guides set A: Management and Planning Set (5 volumes A1-A5)
  ISBN: 0 471 92555 1

- CCTA IS Guides set B: Systems Development Set (8 volumes B1-B8)
  ISBN: 0 471 92556 X

- CCTA IS Guide volume A2: Strategic Planning for Information Systems
  ISBN: 0 471 92522 5

- CCTA IS Guide volume C4: Security and Privacy
  ISBN: 0 471 92537 3

- CCTA IS Guide volume E4: Facilities Management
  ISBN: 0 471 92547 0

Information Systems Engineering Library

The Information Systems Engineering Library volumes, are available from HMSO Books (Dept A), Freepost, Norwich, NR3 1BR, or telephone 071 873 9090, fax 071 873 8200.

The following volumes are referenced in this publication:

- Estimating with Mark II Function Point Analysis
  ISBN: 0 11 330578 8

- Improving the Maintainability of Software
  ISBN: 0 11 330585 0

- Quality Management for PRINCE and SSADM Projects
  ISBN: 011 330580 X

IS Planning Subject Guides

The IS Planning Subject Guides are available from the CCTA Library, CCTA, Riverwalk House, 157-161 Millbank, London SW1P 4RT or telephone 071 217 3331.

IT Infrastructure Library

The IT Infrastructure Library volumes are available from HMSO Books (Dept A), Freepost, Norwich, NR3 1BR, or telephone 071 873 9090, fax 071 873 8200.

The following volumes are referenced in this publication:

- Change Management
  ISBN: 0 11 330525 7

- Configuration Management
  ISBN: 0 11 330530 3

- Help Desk
  ISBN: 0 11 330522 2

- Managing Facilities Management
  ISBN: 0 11 330526 5

- Managing Supplier Relationships
  ISBN: 0 11 330562 1

- Problem Management
  ISBN: 0 11 330527 3

- Service Level Management
  ISBN: 0 11 330521 4

- Software Control and Distribution
  ISBN: 0 11 330537 0

- Software Lifecycle Support
  ISBN: 0 11 330559 1

- Testing an IT Service for Operational Use
  ISBN: 0 11 330560 5

Bibliography

- Third Party and Single Source Maintenance
  ISBN: 0 11 330540 0

Other publications

A Guide to Procurement within the Total Acquisition Process, CCTA, Norwich, 1991.
ISBN: 0 946683 58 1

The Market Testing IS/IT booklets and Management Briefings are available from the CCTA Library, CCTA, Riverwalk House, 157-161 Millbank, London, SW1P 4RT, or telephone 071 217 3331.

White Paper, Competing for Quality, 1991, HMSO (Cm 1730).

Management of Software Maintenance

Glossary

adaptive maintenance	The change made to application software to adapt it for a change of the supporting environment, or network or hardware platform.
amendment testing	The testing of code which is created or altered to implement an amendment to existing software.
CCTA Risk Analysis and Management Method (CRAMM)	A method which provides a structured and consistent basis to identify and justify all the protective measures necessary to ensure the security of both current and future IT systems used for processing data.
corrective maintenance	The correction of processing, performance or implementation problems in application software.
facilities management (FM)	The provision of the management, operation and support of an organisation's IT systems and/or computers and/or networks by an external source at agreed service levels. The service is generally provided for a set time at an agreed cost.
hand-over	The period during which an organisation hands over the running of all or part of its IT service provision to a Facilities Management provider or when a Facilities Management provider is relinquishing the contract to another provider at the end of the contract.
IEEE	Institute of Electrical and Electronics Engineers
IS	Information Systems
IT	Information Technology
logical design	The product of stage 5 of the SSADM software development method.
perfective maintenance	Any modification or enhancement of the existing functionality or performance of application software.
physical design	The product of stage 6 of the SSADM software development method .

preventive maintenance	Action taken to make subsequent maintenance of application software more efficient and reliable.
regression testing	The testing of an application software system or subsystem following amendment of any part of that software, or of software that might interfere with the application software system, using an agreed set of test cases previously developed to test the existing functionality of the software.
reverse engineering	The process of analysing a software subject to identify the system's components and their inter-relationships, and to create representations of the system in another form or at higher levels of abstraction. These representations make the software subject more amenable to enquiry, analysis, re-use and documentation. Reverse engineering may require the use of a repository, or the generation of information in an appropriate form and notation for re-engineering into a new system using CASE tools.
service control team (SCT)	A team of people with skills roughly equivalent to business analysts who will be responsible for managing a service provider on behalf of the user organisation.
service level agreement (SLA)	The written agreement or contract between the customers and the IT service provider which documents the agreed service levels and quality criteria for an IT service.
software maintenance	Any modification of a software product after delivery to correct faults, to improve performance or other attributes or to adapt the product to a changed environment. (IEEE Standard P1219).
Structured Systems Analysis and Design Method (SSADM)	SSADM is a non-proprietary and publicly available method which provides a structured set of procedural, technical and documentation standards designed specifically for analysing business needs and undertaking software development.
third party maintenance (TPM)	The provision of maintenance services by a company which operates independently of the original vendors of the system.